SCHOLASTIC

News

Nonfiction Readers®

Let's Talk Baseball

by Janice Behrens

Children's Press®
An Imprint of Scholastic Inc.
New York Toronto London Auckland Sydney
Mexico City New Delhi Hong Kong
Danbury, Connecticut

These content vocabulary word builders are for grades 1–2.

Subject Consultant: Thomas Sawyer, EdD, Professor of Recreation and Sport Management, Indiana State University

Reading Consultant: Cecilia Minden-Cupp, PhD, Reading Specialist and Author, Chapel Hill, North Carolina

Photographs © 2009: Alamy Images: 5 top right, 18 (Jeff Greenberg), 21 (Erik Isakson/RubberBall), 4 bottom left, 12 (Todd Muskopf); AP Images: 23 top left; Corbis Images: 5 bottom left, 8 (William Manning), 1, 11 (Robert Michael), 17 (Ariel Skelley); Getty Images: back cover, 7 (First Light), 23 bottom left (Hulton Archive), 19 (Jed Jacobsohn), 2, 4 top, 4 bottom right, 14 (Jim McIsaac), 23 bottom right (National Baseball Hall of Fame Library/Major League Baseball), 23 top right (Ezra Shaw); PhotoEdit/ Jeff Greenberg: 13; Robertstock.com/Erik Isakson: 20; Superstock, Inc./Digital Vision Ltd.: 9; VEER: 5 top left, 10, 15 (Patrik Giardino/Flirt Photography), 5 bottom right, 6 (Photodisc Photography), cover (Stockbyte Photography).

Series Design: Simonsays Design!
Book Production: Scholastic Classroom Magazines

Library of Congress Cataloging-in-Publication Data

Behrens, Janice, 1972–
Let's talk baseball / Janice Behrens.
    p. cm.—(Scholastic news nonfiction readers)
Includes bibliographical references and index.
ISBN-13: 978-0-531-13827-4 (lib. bdg.) 978-0-531-20427-6 (pbk.)
ISBN-10: 0-531-13827-5 (lib. bdg.) 0-531-20427-8 (pbk.)
1. Baseball—Juvenile literature. I. Title.
GV867.5.B45 2008
796.357—dc22   2007042012

©2009 Scholastic Inc.
All rights reserved. Published in 2009 by Children's Press, an imprint of Scholastic Inc. Published simultaneously in Canada. Printed in the United States of America.   44
SCHOLASTIC, CHILDREN'S PRESS, and associated logos are trademarks and/or registered trademarks of Scholastic Inc.
1 2 3 4 5 6 7 8 9 10 R 18 17 16 15 14 13 12 11 10 09

CONTENTS

WORD HUNT

Look for these words as you read. They will be in **bold**.

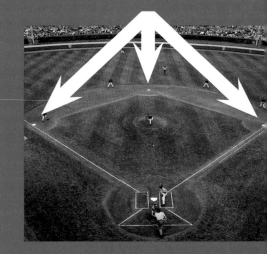

bases
(**bayss**-ez)

fly ball
(flye bawl)

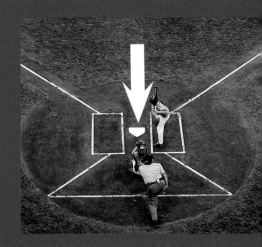

home plate
(home playt)

batter
(**bat**-ur)

fans
(fanz)

pitcher
(**pich**-ur)

umpire
(**uhm**-pire)

Play Ball!

A baseball game is about to begin. The **umpire** says, "Play ball!" The umpire makes sure all the players follow the rules.

umpire

One team bats, while the other team is on the field.

The **pitcher** gets ready to throw the ball. That's called the windup. The best pitchers can throw a ball faster than a speeding car!

pitcher

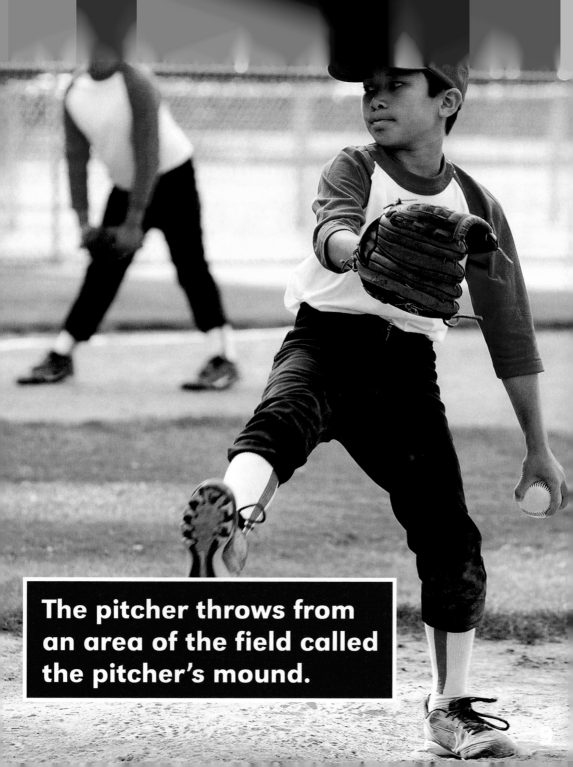

The pitcher throws from an area of the field called the pitcher's mound.

If the **batter** swings and misses the ball, it's called a strike. Three strikes and you're out! That means the batter's turn is over.

batter

If the batter misses, the catcher is there to catch the ball.

Players on the other team try to catch the ball. If someone catches the ball, the batter is out.

Sometimes a batter hits a **fly ball**. That's when the ball goes high in the air.

fly ball

A glove helps players catch the ball.
Without it, catching the ball could hurt!

If no one catches the ball, the batter tries to run around the **bases**. He runs to first, second, and third base. Then comes **home plate**. When the batter gets to home plate, he scores!

bases

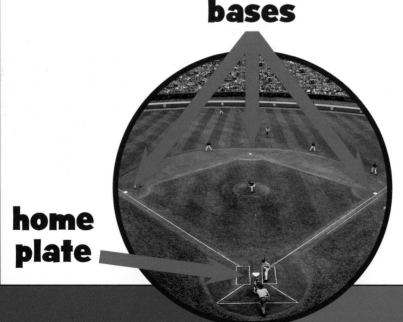

home plate

Sometimes players slide into base.

A slugger is a batter who hits the ball really hard. What happens when a slugger is at bat?

When a slugger swings and hits, you hear a crack!

The sweet spot is the best spot on the bat to hit the ball.

The slugger hits the ball out of the park! He runs around the bases without stopping. That's called a home run.

The **fans** cheer. Their team scored the most runs. They won the game!

fans

CATCHER

Do you know the words for baseball gear?

Catcher's Helmet and Mask

Chest Protector

Mitt

Baseball

Knee and Leg Guards

BATTER

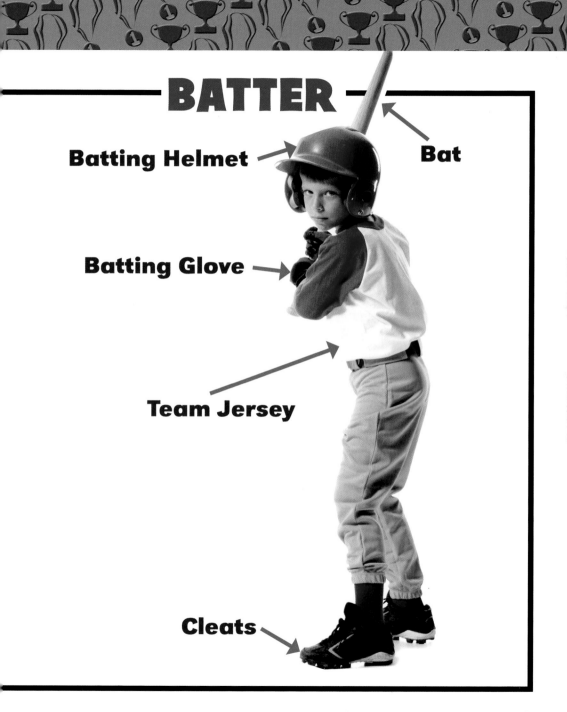

Batting Helmet

Bat

Batting Glove

Team Jersey

Cleats

YOUR NEW WORDS

bases (**bayss**-ez) the four spots on a baseball field you must run to in order to score

batter (**bat**-ur) the player whose turn it is to bat

fans (fanz) people who are wildly enthusiastic about something

fly ball (flye bawl) a ball that goes high in the air when a batter hits it

home plate (home playt) the last base a runner must touch to score a run

pitcher (**pich**-ur) the player who throws the ball to the batter

umpire (**uhm**-pire) the person who rules on plays in baseball and some other sports

FOUR BASEBALL GREATS

Roberto Clemente

Derek Jeter

Jackie Robinson

Babe Ruth

INDEX

FIND OUT MORE

Book:

Smith, Charles R. *Diamond Life: Baseball Sights, Sounds, and Swings.* New York: Orchard Books, 2004.

Website:

The Official Site of Major League Baseball: Kids' Dugout
http://mlb.mlb.com/mlb/kids/index.jsp

MEET THE AUTHOR

Janice Behrens is a writer and Scholastic editor. She and her family live in Brooklyn, New York, where they root for the Yankees.